—SCIENCE—
THROUGH THE
—SEASONS—

SPRING
ON THE FARM

Janet Fitzgerald

Evans Brothers Limited

Acknowledgement

I should like to express my gratitude to the schools, teachers and children with whom I have worked, and with whose help I have gained the experience and confidence needed to write this series. I am particularly indebted to those schools which allowed photographs to be taken as the children carried out their investigations. Thanks are also due to Chris Fairclough for some of the excellent photographs illustrating the texts.

Janet Fitzgerald

The publishers would like to thank the following for supplying photographs for this book:

Ardea 6, 20; Bruce Coleman Ltd front cover, 8, 10, 14, 24; Chris Fairclough back cover, title page, 7, 9, 11-13, 15, 16-19, 21-23, 25; Farmer's Weekly 26, 27.

Author's note

Books in this series are intended for use by young children actively engaged in exploring the environment in the company of a teacher or parent. Many lifelong interests are formed at this early age, and a caring attitude towards plants, animals and resources can be nurtured to become a mature concern for conservation in general.

The basis for all scientific investigation rests on the ability to observe closely and to ask questions. These books aim to increase a child's awareness so that he or she learns to make accurate observations. First-hand experience is encouraged and simple investigations of observations are suggested. The child will suggest many more! The aim is to give children a broad base of experience and 'memories' on which to build for the future.

The books in this series meet the requirements of the National Curriculum for Science. In particular they support:

Key Stage One
Attainment target 1: Scientific investigations

Attainment target 2: Life and Living processes

The extension activities are wide and challenging and would adequately prepare children for work within Key Stage Two.

The books support scientific investigation in AT1 by encouraging children to:
• ask questions
• observe, compare and measure
• interpret observations

Through real life situations children are encouraged to sort, group and describe materials and events in their immediate environment. Questions are suggested and ideas presented which lead to predictions based on everyday experiences, which can be tested. The tasks encourage the children to go beyond a description of what they observe and to give a simple explanation of how and why it happened.

For AT2 the material supports the study of plants and animals in a variety of local environments and begins to explore the basic life processes common to humans and other animals.

Published by Evans Brothers Limited
2A Portman Mansions
Chiltern Street
London W1M 1LE

First published in Great Britain in 1989 by
Hamish Hamilton Children's Books

First published 1989
Reprinted 1994

British Library Cataloguing-in-Publication Data
    Fitzgerald, Janet
        Spring on the farm
        1. Agricultural industries.
          Farms – For children
        I. Title II. Series
        338.1

Printed in Spain by GRAFO, S.A. - Bilbao

ISBN 0 237 60220 2

Contents

It is spring on the farm and

                                      cows eat new grass.

Now that the weather is warmer cows can graze.

Look at the fresh green colour of the grass.

What other plants might grow in the grass?

How can you tell if grass
is beginning to grow?

Put three hoops on the grass
in different places.

Draw what is growing in the hoops each week.

What has happened to the grass after four weeks?

It is spring on the farm and

hens sit on eggs.

The hen keeps the eggs safe and warm.

It helps the eggs to hatch.

How is the hen using her feathers?

To incubate eggs we need a warm safe place.
The eggs must be turned every day.

How many days do the eggs need to be
in the incubator?

How can we tell if all the eggs
have been turned?

It is spring on the farm and

chicks are hatched.

What are the chicks doing?

Why is the farmyard a good place for chicks?

Is the mother hen looking after them?

Chicks must be carefully looked after.
They need food and water.

What do chicks like to eat?
How often should they be given fresh water?

It is spring on the farm and ducklings look for water.

How many ducklings can you see?

Are they all doing the same thing?

Are the ducklings the same shape as their mother?

At first ducklings are fluffy.

Later they grow special feathers.

Look at some small fluffy feathers.

Look at some large stiff feathers.

Put the feathers into a bowl of water.

Watch what happens.

It is spring on the farm and swallows fly to the barn.

Look at the shape of the swallow.

Will the shape help the bird to fly?

What is the swallow looking for?

More birds visit gardens when the weather gets warmer.

Look out of the window at the same time every day.

Can you see any of these birds?

Which bird do you see most often?

It is spring on the farm and

crops are sown.

Look at the patterns made by the tractor.

Why are the seeds sown in rows?

Collect some grains of wheat, barley and oats.

Plant the seeds in different pots.

Water them carefully.

Measure the shoots to see
how quickly they grow.

It is spring on the farm and rabbits eat young shoots.

What is the rabbit doing in the field?

Does the farmer like the rabbit?

How will the rabbit know when the farmer is coming?

Rabbits know when danger is near because they can hear very well.

Look at the shape of the animals' ears.

Which animals will be able to hear very well?

Put your hands behind your ears to make them seem bigger.

Can you hear better?

It is spring on the farm and
lambs are born.

Sometimes lambs are born when it is very cold.

How will they find shelter?

Who will help the lambs?

Sometimes sheep's wool gets stuck
to a fence or hedge.

See if you can find some.

What does the wool feel like?

What happens if you put the wool into water?

Wash the wool in warm water with some soap.

What has changed?

It is spring on the farm and
sheep dogs are working.

What is the sheep dog trying to do?

Where does he want the sheep to go?

How do the sheep know what to do?

Ask your friends if they have a dog.

Collect pictures of different dogs.

Look at the fur, ears and head of the dogs.

Are they different?

Which dogs are most like sheep dogs?

It is spring on the farm and
barn owls have their young.

Where has the mother owl made her nest?

Why is this a good place for owls?

What has the parent bird brought
for the young birds to eat?

Birds are busy in spring
feeding their young.

Look at the shape of the beaks
of the young birds.

How will this shape help the parent birds?

Find out what sort of food
the parent will bring.

Looking at . . .

. . . different farms

There are many different kinds of farms.

Some are large and some are small.

Some farmers keep animals.

Some farmers grow crops, like wheat and potatoes.

Try to find out more about different farms.

For teachers and parents

We all recognise that children possess an insatiable curiosity about the rich environment and exciting experiences around them. For this reason they have a natural affinity for science and a basic inclination to explore and discover the world in which we live. We need to foster this sense of wonder by encouraging a scientific way of thinking in the early years. Children's own experience of the immediate environment will provide a natural starting point.

Through science children can evolve an active process of enquiry. This begins with observation (including sorting, comparing, ordering and measuring) and continues with asking questions, devising practical investigations, predicting outcomes, controlling variables, noting results, and perhaps modifying the original question in the light of discovery. The books in this series offer suggestions for engaging young children in this sort of active enquiry by relating seasonal change to familiar surroundings.

Extension activities

Pages 6–7
Examine the variety of other plants in the grass and measure the rate of growth. Many of the plants will be low growing with rosette type leaves (e.g. daisy, dandelion, buttercup, plantain, clover). These plants tend to spread horizontally over the ground in order to escape the first mowings. Notice when the first flower buds begin to appear and how the the roots of the grasses thicken and growth accelerates as hours of daylight increase and temperatures rise.

Pages 8–9
Refer to books and diagrams to discover what is happening inside the egg during incubation. With care, it is possible to see the developing embryo inside the egg by holding it in front of a strong light. Find out why the eggs need to be turned every day if an incubator is used. If it is possible to study the behaviour of a broody hen, discover how often she leaves the eggs, when and how she feeds and drinks and how she ensures that all the eggs are warm.

Pages 10–11

Investigate the food chicks need to eat in the early days after hatching. How much do they eat at first, after a week and after a month? Does the type of food change? Monitor the rate of growth by measuring and weighing. The latter can be achieved by gently placing the chick in a small fabric bag and suspending it from a spring balance. Notice any changes of colour in feet or beak. Watch out for changes in feathers, from the early fluffy ones to flight feathers.

Pages 12–13

If possible compare chicks with ducklings. Both are easy to incubate. Look at beaks and feet and consider differences in feeding and other behaviour. Compare size, weight and body shape. Look at the position and shape of the wings. If possible look for the development of feathers and the oil gland.

Pages 14–15

Choose an appropriate viewing point and record the number of birds seen at different times of the day. Make charts to show numbers and species. Watch one specific bird move from perching points to feeding points. (A robin is a good bird to choose.) Make a drawing to show the flight pattern. Watch thrushes, blackbirds and starlings feeding on the lawn or school field. Do they all feed together?

Pages 16–17

Investigate different grains. Bird seed is easy to get and contains many different seeds. Sort out the wheat, oats and barley which the farmer will plant either in autumn or spring. Try growing some of the other seeds. Compare the shoots for rate of growth and shape of leaves. Plant a handful of seeds very close together to see which seeds produce the strongest shoots. Look at the problems farmers face growing crops in different climates. Discuss drought, famine and irrigation.

Pages 18–19

Investigate ways to make our hearing more effective. The plastic cup and string telephone is one way. Discover how sounds travel through solids and liquids. Find out how far voices travel without help. Try to find ways to make sounds travel further.

Pages 20–21

Collect different samples of wool. Look closely at the strands of the wool. Test to see if the wool will stretch and if it will retain its shape. Discuss why we need different thicknesses of wool for special purposes (e.g. babies' clothes, hikers' socks). Try dying sheep's wool using vegetable dyes (e.g. onion, elderberry, beetroot). Compare these colours with synthetic dyes.

Pages 22–23

Find out if different breeds of dogs have similar behaviour patterns. Do they all need the same amount of exercise? Do they eat the same type of food even if they have different quantities? Discuss special breeds of dog for specific jobs (e.g. police dogs, guard dogs, dogs for the blind).

Pages 24–25

If possible, identify a place where a parent bird is feeding young. Being very careful not to disturb them, watch to see how the parent bird approaches the nest. Is it the same every time? Do the fledglings make more noise as the parent bird approaches? How many times in an hour does the bird return? Is it possible to see what food it is carrying? Notice the site chosen for the nest. Is it well camouflaged, with easy access? Is it high enough to be safe from cats? How will the fledglings get out of the nest?

Index